HORSES

The ARABIAN Horse

by Carrie A. Braulick

Consultant:
Molly Benstein
Communications Assistant
Arabian Horse Association (AHA)
Aurora, Colorado

Capstone press

Mankato, Minnesota

Edge Books are published by Capstone Press,
151 Good Counsel Drive, P.O. Box 669, Mankato, Minnesota 56002.
www.capstonepress.com

Library of Congress Cataloging-in-Publication Data
Braulick, Carrie A., 1975–
    The Arabian horse / by Carrie A. Braulick.
    p. cm.—(Edge books. Horses)
    Includes bibliographical references (p. 31) and index.
    ISBN 0-7368-3765-5 (hardcover)
    1. Arabian horse—Juvenile literature. I. Title. II. Series.
SF293.A8B73 2005
636.1'12—dc22   2004019413

Summary: Describes the Arabian horse, including its history, physical features,
and uses today.

Credits
Juliette Peters, designer; Deirdre Barton, photo researcher; Scott Thoms,
    photo editor

Photo Credits
Artiques, LTD/Ann Hatchett-Sprague, 5
Capstone Press/Deirdre Barton, back cover; Gary Sundermeyer (objects), 8,
    15, 20
Courtesy of Dr. Leo Cuello (the owner of Cass Olé), 14
© 1999 Genie Stewart-Spears, 19, 23
© 2002 Genie Stewart-Spears, 22
Javan Photography, cover
Karen Patterson, 13
Library of Congress, 9
© 2004 Mark J. Barrett, 6, 11, 16–17, 25, 29
Paula da Silva, 21, 26

**Capstone Press thanks Diane Fralish, owner of Riverwind Saddle & Tack,
for providing the endurance saddle used as an artistic effect in this book.**

1 2 3 4 5 6 10 09 08 07 06 05

Table of Contents

Chapter 1

A Long History

The Bedouin people have lived in the deserts of the Middle East for at least 2,000 years. Early Bedouins formed strong bonds with their horses. They trained the horses to fight in wars. Sometimes, they let the horses live with them in their tents. But the Bedouins weren't happy with just any type of horse. They rode only Arabians.

Today's Arabian owners have the same passion for their horses that the Bedouins did. Arabians are one of the world's most popular horse breeds.

Learn about:
- ★ **The Bedouins**
- ★ **Muhammad**
- ★ **Arabians in North America**

Early Bedouins were well known for their obedient Arabian horses.

▲ Today, people sometimes ride Arabians in outfits based on the Bedouins' clothing.

Early Beginnings

The Arabian is the oldest horse breed. No one knows exactly when the breed began. Ancient Egyptian artwork from around 1300 BC shows horse drawings that look like today's Arabians. The ancient Egyptians may have used Arabians to pull chariots in wars.

Early Bedouins are known for starting the first Arabian breeding programs. They carefully selected the horses they bred. They wanted to produce the best war horses.

Religion and Royalty

By the AD 600s, the religion of Islam had gained popularity in the Middle East. Islam's founder, Muhammad, raised Arabians. Mounted on Arabian horses, Muhammad and his followers spread the Islam religion.

An Arabian Legend

Muhammad's interest in Arabians was so well known that people told stories about it. One story says that Muhammad once locked up about 100 Arabian mares. He didn't give them water for three days. Muhammad then let the horses run loose. All the horses ran toward a nearby pool of water. Muhammad then blew a battle horn. The horn's sound meant that the horses were needed for war. Most of the horses kept on running. But five mares stopped, turned around, and returned to Muhammad. The story says that these five mares helped start the Arabian horse breed.

The success of Arabians as war horses made them valuable. From the 1200s to the 1800s, many Middle Eastern rulers had large Arabian farms. They sent people far into the desert to find the best Arabian horses.

The Breed Spreads

By the late 1800s, people in European countries wanted Arabians. In 1881, Wilfred and Anne Blunt brought several Arabian horses from the Middle East to England. They started a large Arabian farm called Crabbet Park. People also started Arabian farms in Germany, Poland, and Hungary.

Arabians also found homes on the other side of the Atlantic Ocean. In 1877, Turkish leaders sent a gift of two Arabian stallions to U.S. President Ulysses S. Grant. These horses were part of one of the first U.S. Arabian breeding programs. In 1906, Homer Davenport brought 27 Arabians from the Middle East to the United States.

The AHA

American owners of Arabians wanted to keep track of their horses' ancestries. In 1908, the Arabian Horse Club of America formed. Later, the registry was renamed the Arabian Horse Association (AHA). By 1950, about 5,000 horses were registered with the AHA. Today, at least 600,000 Arabians are registered with the AHA.

Ulysses S. Grant received the Arabian stallion Leopard in 1877.

Chapter 2

Not Just a Pretty Face

Today, many horse breeds look different from Arabians. Yet nearly all horses have Arabian ancestors. Early horse breeders admired the Arabian's look and skill. They mated Arabians with other types of horses.

Basic Features

Arabians can have gray, bay, chestnut, black, or roan coats. Bay coats are red-brown. All bay horses have black manes and tails. Chestnut coats are a copper color. Roan Arabians have bay, black, or chestnut coats with a mixture of white hair. Like other horses, Arabians may have white leg and face markings.

Learn about:
★ Colors
★ Size
★ Personality

Arabians have a proud look and a free, long stride.

Horses are measured from the ground to the withers, or top of the shoulders. Arabians usually are between 14.2 and 15.2 hands high. A hand equals 4 inches (10 centimeters). Many other breeds are taller. But Arabians can carry a great deal of weight for their size.

A Graceful Horse

Many people think the Arabian is the most beautiful of all horse breeds. It is known for its graceful features. The Arabian has a long curved neck. Its sloped shoulders are in front of a short, strong back. The Arabian often has a long, full mane and tail. It carries its tail higher than other horses do.

People say the Arabian seems to float as it moves. It steps lightly with long, free strides.

The Arabian's Head

The Arabian's head is one of its most striking features. The small head slopes inward below the eyes. The slope creates a low spot, or dish. The Arabian's large, dark eyes are spaced far apart from each other. Its ears are small and pointed.

The Arabian's head angles down to a small, soft muzzle. Some people say its muzzle looks like it can fit into a teacup.

The dish below the eyes is one of the Arabian's well-known features.

Made to Run

Arabians can run long distances without tiring. They have large nostrils that can take in a great deal of air. For their size, Arabians have a deep chest. The chest allows the lungs to enlarge and hold the air brought in through the nostrils.

Cass Olé learned to rear for the movie *The Black Stallion*.

Arabians also have strong leg bones to help them run long distances. Healthy Arabians that aren't overworked usually have few leg injuries.

Personality

Arabians are more lively and sensitive than most other breeds. Some people think the Arabian's personality makes it hard to train. But Arabians that are handled properly behave well.

The intelligence of Arabians helps them learn quickly. In the late 1970s, an Arabian horse named Cass Olé played the starring role in the movie *The Black Stallion*. In only 11 weeks, Cass Olé learned to paw, rear, lie down, and perform several other stunts.

Arabians are known to bond well with people. Many horse owners believe Arabians sense people's feelings better than other horses can. Managers of riding programs for people with disabilities often choose Arabians because of these qualities.

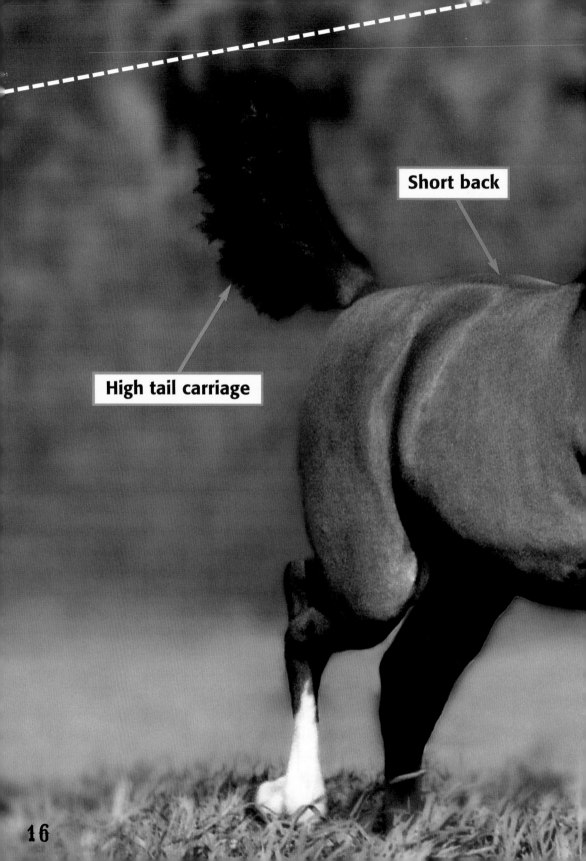

Short back

High tail carriage

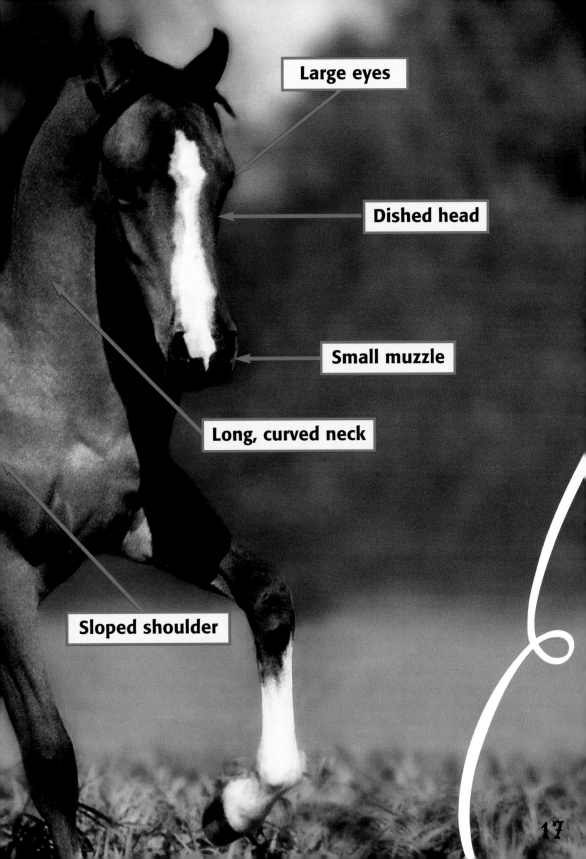

Large eyes

Dished head

Small muzzle

Long, curved neck

Sloped shoulder

17

Chapter 3

Champions of Endurance

The Arabian's ability to travel long distances without tiring makes it a perfect choice for endurance racing. Riders use more Arabians in endurance races than any other breed.

Endurance Races

The American Endurance Ride Conference (AERC) runs most endurance races in the United States and Canada. AERC races are 50 to 100 miles (80 to 161 kilometers) long. Beginners sometimes compete in 25-mile (40-kilometer) races.

Learn about:
* ★ AERC races
* ★ Checkpoints
* ★ Training for endurance races

Arabians are the most suitable horses for endurance racing.

Arabians do well in endurance races even on the roughest types of land. The Tevis Cup race covers parts of the Sierra Nevada Mountains in California. Throughout the ride, horses climb at least 15,000 feet (4,600 meters). Since the first Tevis Cup in 1955, all of the winners except two were partbred or purebred Arabians.

Physical Condition

Endurance racing horses must be in good physical condition. Endurance races have vet checks, or checkpoints. At each checkpoint, veterinarians make sure each horse is fit to continue the race. They check the horse's pulse and breathing rate. They also make sure the horse's legs are not injured.

The first 10 horses that finish a race can compete in the best condition judging. Veterinarians consider the time of race completion and the horse's physical condition to decide on a winner. They also consider the amount of weight the horse carried.

FACT

A horse in a 50-mile (80-kilometer) endurance race can lose about 10 gallons (38 liters) of water by sweating.

At checkpoints, race workers sometimes cool down the horses with water.

21

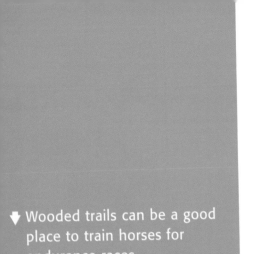

Wooded trails can be a good place to train horses for endurance races.

Training

Training for endurance racing can take several years. Horses competing at national or international levels usually have at least three years of endurance training.

People training horses for endurance racing work their horses often. Many people ride their horses several times each week.

Beginning endurance riders start training by going on short rides. At first, rides should be no longer than 3 miles (4.8 kilometers). Horses can slowly work up to rides 15 to 25 miles (24 to 40 kilometers) long.

Riders teach their horses to trot at a steady, fast pace. A steady, fast trot helps horses use more oxygen.

Earle Baxter

Earle Baxter is a top endurance rider. Since 1978, he has ridden at least 19,000 miles (30,600 kilometers) on endurance rides. In 1989 and 1998, he was a U.S. national champion. In 1991, he competed in the North American Championship race on the Canadian team. The team won the gold medal. In 2002, he was inducted into the AERC Hall of Fame.

After three to nine months, horses may be ready for more advanced training. Riders can start cantering, or running, more often. They also may start traveling over rough land or hills.

Chapter 4

Arabians in Action

People who train their horses for endurance riding can compete in many races. Most of these races are local or regional. Top riders compete at national and international levels. International races include the Pan American Endurance Championships and the World Endurance Championships.

Shows

Endurance racing is not the only talent of Arabians. Arabians are popular show horses. Some people show Arabians at open shows with other breeds. Other people compete at shows only for Arabians.

Learn about:
- ★ Horse shows
- ★ Arabian racing
- ★ Owning an Arabian

Arabian horse racing is becoming more popular in the United States.

Some Arabians compete in jumping events.

At shows, events are divided into classes. People ride their horses in many classes. In halter classes, handlers lead their horses by a halter. Horses are judged on their physical features and their ability to stand in a show position.

Other Events

Crowds go wild when they watch Thoroughbreds speed around a track. Arabian racing is less popular, but it is still exciting. The Arabian Cup Championships is the largest U.S. Arabian race.

In 2003, the AHA held its first Sport Horse National Arabian and Half-Arabian Championship. Sport horses compete in jumping and do advanced moves in a riding style called dressage.

Owning an Arabian

Owning a horse is a big responsibility. Like all horses, Arabians need a great deal of care. Owners must provide food, water, and shelter. Arabians also need large, open spaces to exercise.

Arabian owners often keep their horses at their farms or stables. Some owners pay to have their horses stay at another person's stable. These boarding fees can be expensive.

A Beloved Breed

Arabians are just as treasured today by their owners as they were by the Bedouins long ago. The classy appearance and talent of the world's oldest breed are sure to keep attracting new owners and riders.

Fast Facts:
The Arabian Horse

History: The Arabian horse breed began in the Arabian Peninsula in southwestern Asia. The Bedouins used them as war horses in the desert. In the 1800s, people brought Arabians to Europe, North America, and other parts of the world.

Height: Arabians are 14.2 to 15.2 hands (about 5 feet or 1.5 meters) tall at the withers. Each hand equals 4 inches (10 centimeters).

Weight: 800 to 1,100 pounds (360 to 500 kilograms)

Colors: bay, gray, chestnut, black, roan

Features: dished head; large eyes; small, pointed ears; long, curved neck; small muzzle; short, straight back; high tail carriage

Personality: lively, intelligent, loyal

Abilities: Arabians are known for their endurance. They are able to carry heavy loads over long distances. Most top endurance racing horses are Arabians. Arabians also are good show and trail horses.

Life span: about 25 to 30 years

Glossary

ancestor (AN-sess-tur)—a member of a breed that lived a long time ago

breed (BREED)—to mate animals so they will produce young; breed also means a group of animals that have the same features and ancestry.

canter (KAN-tur)—a gait of a horse that is faster than the trot and slower than the gallop

dressage (druh-SAHJ)—a riding style in which horses complete a pattern while doing advanced moves

endurance (en-DUR-enss)—the ability to keep doing an activity for long periods of time

mare (MAIR)—an adult female horse

registry (REH-juh-stree)—an organization that keeps track of the ancestry for horses of a certain breed

stallion (STAL-yuhn)—an adult male horse that can be used for breeding

withers (WITH-urs)—the top of a horse's shoulders

Read More

Barnes, Julia. *101 Facts about Horses and Ponies.*
101 Facts about Pets. Milwaukee: Gareth Stevens, 2002.

Kelley, Brent P. *Horse Breeds of the World.* The Horse
Library. Philadelphia: Chelsea House, 2002.

Murray, Julie. *Arabian Horses.* Animal Kingdom. Edina,
Minn.: Abdo, 2003.

Internet Sites

FactHound offers a safe, fun way to find Internet sites
related to this book. All of the sites on FactHound have been
researched by our staff.

Here's how:

1. Visit *www.facthound.com*
2. Type in this special code **0736837655** for
   age-appropriate sites. Or enter a search word
   related to this book for a more general search.
3. Click on the **Fetch It** button.

FactHound will fetch the best sites for you!

Index